THE ROMAN EMPIRE

Peter Chrisp

Wayland

Themes in History

The American Frontier
The Crusades
The French Revolution and Napoleon
Life in the Middle Ages
The Rise of Islam
The Roman Empire

Cover Illustration:
The equestrian statue of Marcus Aurelius on the Capitoline Hill in Rome

First published in 1991 by
Wayland (Publishers) Limited
61 Western Road, Hove
East Sussex BN3 1JD, England

Editor: Mike Hirst
Designer: Joyce Chester
Consultant: Dr Jamie Masters, Research Fellow in Classics,
Clare College, Cambridge.

British Library Cataloguing in Publication Data

Chrisp, Peter
The Roman Empire. – (Themes in history)
I. Title   II. Series
936

ISBN 0 7502 0199 1

Typeset by Dorchester Typesetting Group Ltd
Printed and bound in Italy by
L.E.G.O. S.p.A., Vicenza

Contents

What was the Roman Empire?

The English word 'empire' comes from '*imperium*', a word used by the Romans. It means 'power' or 'authority'. Throughout history, some nations have gained power over other peoples, usually by winning wars. Some of these powerful nations have managed to control large parts of the earth. A vast area under the control of one nation is called an empire.

One of the most successful empires was that based in the city of ancient Rome. The Roman Empire lasted for several hundred years, from the third century BC to the fifth century AD. At its height in the second century AD, it stretched 4,000 km east to west and 3,700 km north to south. For the only

The Roman Empire was at its greatest extent in AD 117, under the Emperor Trajan.

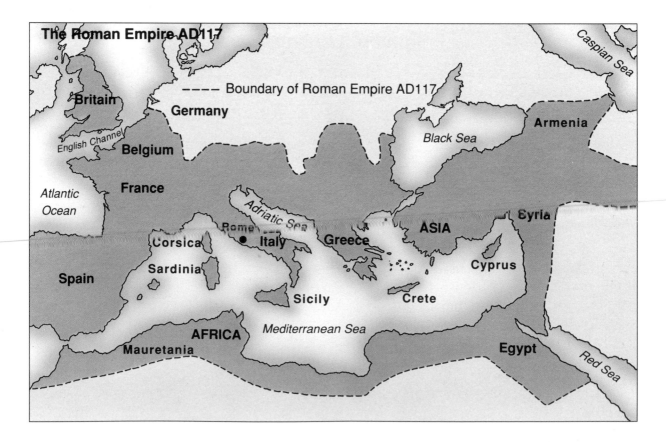

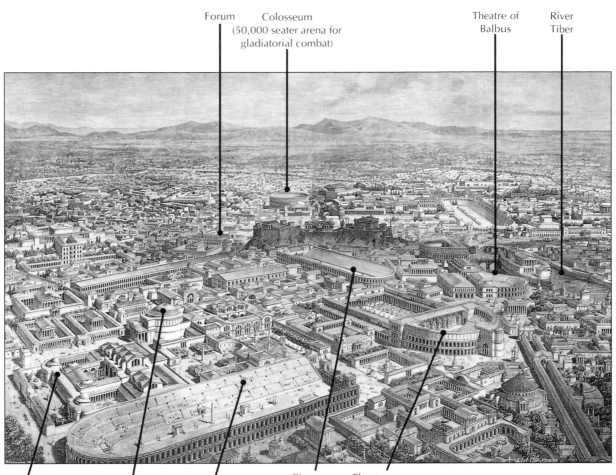

Forum

Colosseum
(50,000 seater arena for
gladiatorial combat)

Theatre of
Balbus

River
Tiber

Baths of
Nero

Pantheon
(Temple dedicated
to all the gods)

Stadium of
Domitian
(chariot racing)

Circus
Flaminius
(chariot
racing)

Theatre
of Pompey
(40,000
seater)

An artist's impression of what Rome would have looked like in AD 270. The city is filled with enormous public buildings – temples, theatres, bath houses and stadia for chariot racing.

time in history, all the lands around the Mediterranean were controlled by a single state. The Romans called the Mediterranean 'our sea'.

Within the Empire, people of many races shared a similar way of life. In places as far apart as Britain and north Africa, Spain and Syria, people used the same type of pottery. They followed Roman fashions, worshipped Roman gods and used Roman money. In the western half of the Empire, they were encouraged to speak Latin. In the east, most people spoke Greek. People who served the Empire well were rewarded by being made Roman citizens. As citizens, they could follow careers in government. Some of the Empire's later rulers were not even from Rome, but came from Spain or Africa.

Right *The Romans supplied their towns with running water, carried along aqueducts. They used the brick arch, a structure which can carry great weight. The water travelled through a concrete channel at the top. This aqueduct, from Segovia in Spain, is 800 m long and 36 m high at its highest point; built around AD 100, it is still in working order.*

Above *Throughout the Empire, people worshipped the Roman gods. This mask of Juno, the goddess of mothers, was found in Hungary.*

In all the countries they conquered, the Romans built towns. They introduced town life to northern Europe – before the Romans, everyone had lived in villages. Each Roman town had its own public meeting place, or forum. This was a place for local government, trade, law and religious festivals. Towns also had places for relaxation – public baths and theatres.

As their power increased, the Romans built a network of straight, paved roads to control their huge Empire. The roads were designed so that Roman armies could travel quickly in any weather. The roads were also used by official messengers carrying orders and news. At regular intervals, there were stations where a messenger could swap a tired horse for a fresh one. People and goods also travelled by water – sea, river and canal. Ships sailed throughout the Empire, carrying grain and olive oil from north Africa, glass from Syria and wool from Britain.

The Romans believed they had a right to conquer other nations. But the peoples they defeated often resented Roman government.

A Roman historian called Tacitus wrote an account of the conquest of northern Britain. At one point, Tacitus imagined a speech that a defeated Briton might make:

A rich enemy excites Roman greed; a poor one their lust for power. To robbery and butchery, they give the lying name of 'government'. They create desolation and call it peace. Our goods and money are swallowed by taxation. Our land is stripped of its harvest to fill their granaries. Our bodies are crippled by building roads through forests and swamps under the lash of our oppressors.

(Tacitus, *Agricola*)

Roman rule was not always unpopular. Some areas asked Rome for protection. A Greek philosopher called Aelius Aristides welcomed Roman rule. He wrote a speech addressed to the Roman nation:

The coasts and interiors have been filled with cities. Now it is possible for Greek and non-Greek to travel wherever he will. For security it is enough to be a Roman citizen, or rather one of those united under your rule. You have spanned the rivers with bridges and dug highways through the mountains. You have accustomed all areas to a settled and orderly way of life. (Aristides, *Roman Oration*)

What were the advantages and disadvantages of Roman rule mentioned by these two authors?

The city of Rome depended on grain imported from Sicily and Africa. This painting from Ostia, Rome's nearest port, shows a boat, the Isis Giminia, *being loaded with grain before travelling up the River Tiber to Rome. The captain, Farnaces, stands at the stern holding the steering oar. In the centre, a man pours corn from a sack while another measures out the quantity.*

Prisoners captured in battle would be sold as slaves.

The Romans claimed that they brought peace and civilization to the lands they conquered. But they also imposed taxes, to pay for their armies and building programmes. The people they captured in battle were usually forced to become slaves. As a result of the taxes in the provinces, the city of Rome grew richer and larger. In the first century AD it had more than a million inhabitants.

The Growth of Rome

In the sixth century BC, Italy was a country of many different peoples and languages. The Romans were just one of the Latin-speaking peoples of central Italy. North of the Latin area was the land of the Etruscans. At first, Rome was dominated by this more civilized people, and under their influence, Rome grew from a small farming settlement into a large city.

Around 510 BC, the Romans felt strong enough to break free of Etruscan rule. But the newly-independent city was surrounded by enemies, and the Romans had to fight for their survival – against Etruscans, other Latins, Celts and other peoples. Sometimes Rome was defeated. In 390 BC, the city was captured by Celtic invaders from the north. The Celts destroyed much of the city and had to be bought off with gold. Yet, despite this setback, Rome survived and gradually extended its power.

One reason for Rome's success was its skill in dealing with other peoples. Instead of trying to destroy rivals, the Romans preferred to make alliances with them. Some loyal allies were given Roman citizenship. In the areas they conquered the Romans also founded colonies – new cities which spread the Latin language and Roman way of life.

Above *A bronze statuette of an Etruscan warrior from the fifth century BC.*

Below *In this scene from the Arch of Constantine, Roman soldiers besiege the city of Verona.*

The earliest Romans could not read or write, so we know very little of their history. Archaeologists have discovered that the city of Rome began as two separate peasant settlements around 850 BC. The Romans themselves claimed that their city had been founded in 753 BC by Romulus, son of the war god Mars. Romulus reigned for thirty-seven years; then, it was said, his father took him to heaven in a fiery chariot. A Roman writer called Livy said:

If any nation deserves the privilege of claiming a divine ancestry, it is our own. The glory won by the Roman people in their wars is so great that, when they declare that Mars himself was their first parent, all the nations of the world should accept their claim.

(Livy, *History*)

Why do you think the Romans wanted to believe that their founder was the son of Mars?

The Roman god of war, Mars. People prayed to Mars for success in war.

A second reason for Rome's expansion was the effectiveness of the Roman Army. Originally, the Romans copied the Etruscan way of fighting. They used a long battle line called a phalanx. The phalanx was a living wall of heavily-armed foot-soldiers, advancing in tight formation. The disadvantage of the phalanx was that it could be used only on open ground. The Romans themselves invented a more flexible method. They broke up their army into smaller units called maniples, each of around 120 men. The Roman army could then split up to attack the enemy from more than one direction at once. Unlike a phalanx, the maniples could also fight off attacks from both the front and rear.

By 270 BC, Rome was in control of the whole of Italy. This expansion brought Rome into conflict with the empire of Carthage in north Africa. The Carthaginians were a race of seafaring traders. With their huge fleet, they controlled the western Mediterranean. They had colonies in southern Spain, Sardinia and Sicily.

According to legend, Rome's founder, Romulus, and his brother Remus were abandoned as babies and suckled by a she-wolf. In this scene from an altar, the twins are about to be discovered by shepherds. The figure at the bottom right represents the River Tiber.

Rome and Carthage first quarrelled, over Sicily, in 264 BC. The result was a war lasting twenty-four years.

In order to fight Carthage, Rome had to build a navy. The Romans were a farming people who knew nothing about the sea. But they got hold of a stranded Carthaginian warship, and copied it to build their own fleet. The Carthaginian method of fighting was to sink a ship by ramming it. Because they were such good sailors, they could always beat the Romans using this method. But the Romans found a way of fighting back. They invented grappling hooks, which could be thrown and used to pull an enemy ship alongside. Then the Roman infantry would leap on to the enemy ship and fight using traditional methods. In 241 BC, the Roman fleet won a decisive victory. Carthage was forced to beg for peace and give up Sicily.

In 218 BC, Hannibal, the young Carthaginian general, led his army through Spain, France and over the Alps, attacking Italy from the north. For fifteen years, his army roamed at large through Italy. This was the greatest threat ever experienced by the Romans.

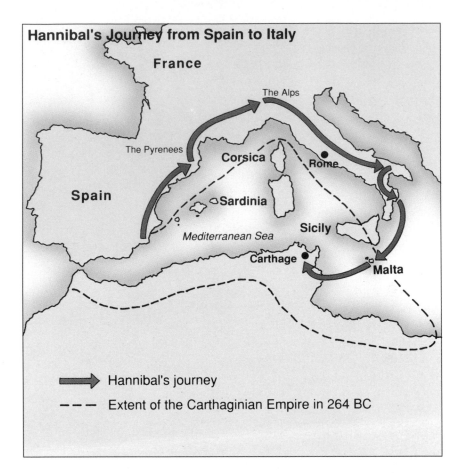

Hannibal's Journey from Spain to Italy

France

The Alps

The Pyrenees

Corsica

Rome

Spain

Sardinia

Sicily

Mediterranean Sea

Carthage

Malta

➡ Hannibal's journey

– – – Extent of the Carthaginian Empire in 264 BC

Why were Rome's armies so successful? A Greek writer called Polybius tried to answer this question in his history of the Roman Empire. He said:

As soon as they saw Greek weapons, the Romans began to copy them. This is one of their strong points: no people is more willing to adopt new customs and to copy what they see is done better by others. (Polybius, *Histories*)

The question was also answered by a Jewish writer called Josephus. He had fought against the Romans in AD 66, when the Jews rebelled against Roman rule. Here is an extract from a book he wrote, in which he explains why the Romans had won:

Roman battle drills are no different from the real thing. Every man works as hard at his daily training as if he was on active service. This is why they stand up so well to the strain of battle. No indiscipline dislodges them from their formations, no panic weakens them, no work wears them out. Victory over less-trained men follows as a matter of course. Training methods are partly based on fear; for military law demands the death penalty not only for leaving a post, but even for minor offences. (Josephus, *The Jewish War*)

Carthage and Rome went to war a second time in 218 BC. A brilliant Carthaginian general called Hannibal led an army, including thirty-seven elephants, across Spain, France and the Alps, attacking Italy from the north. Hannibal hoped that the cities of central Italy would rise against Rome. But although he won several victories, most of Rome's allies stayed loyal. Hannibal was eventually beaten in 202 BC.

Fifty years later, Rome decided to destroy Carthage once and for all. After a three-year siege, the city was burned to the ground and its inhabitants made slaves. Rome inherited Carthage's empire.

Having conquered the western Mediterranean, Rome turned east. Between 197 and 146 BC, the Romans conquered Syria and Greece. However, this was not a deliberate plan of conquest. Often, small states asked Rome for help when they were attacked by larger states. The Romans increasingly saw themselves as peacemakers; they thought it was their duty to sort out other peoples' quarrels. In Greece, it seemed that the only way to stop the cities fighting each other was to impose Roman rule.

Roman soldiers cross a river on a temporary bridge, made by lashing boats together.

At the Empire's frontiers, the Romans built defensive barriers and forts. This is Hadrian's Wall, built in north Britain about AD 122.

Next, the Romans conquered the lands of the Celts – northern Spain (133 BC), Gaul (modern France) (120–50 BC) and Britain (AD 43). The Romans believed that the Celts were uncivilized barbarians. They argued that they were doing the Celts a favour by giving them Roman civilization.

The Roman Republic

At first, Rome was ruled by kings. According to tradition, the last king of Rome was a cruel and ruthless man called Tarquin the Proud. In 510 BC, a group of Roman nobles rebelled against Tarquin and drove him out. They set up a republic: a state without a king. The Romans were determined that they would never again allow one man to have unlimited power. So they invented a system of government to prevent it happening.

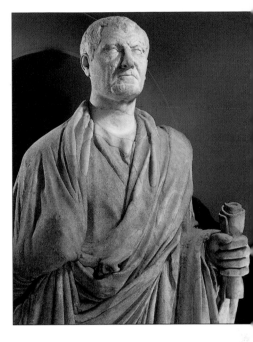

Above *A statue of a Consul, the highest official in the Republic.*

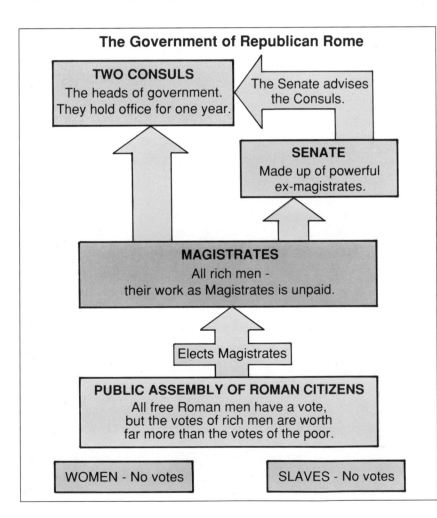

The Government of Republican Rome

TWO CONSULS
The heads of government.
They hold office for one year.

The Senate advises the Consuls.

SENATE
Made up of powerful ex-magistrates.

MAGISTRATES
All rich men -
their work as Magistrates is unpaid.

Elects Magistrates

PUBLIC ASSEMBLY OF ROMAN CITIZENS
All free Roman men have a vote,
but the votes of rich men are worth
far more than the votes of the poor.

WOMEN - No votes

SLAVES - No votes

Left *This diagram shows how the rulers of the Roman Republic were chosen. Women and slaves had no political rights.*

In 63 BC, the Consul Cicero unmasked a plot by a noble called Catiline to overthrow the Republic. In this dramatic nineteenth-century painting, Cicero attacks Catiline in the Senate. Catiline sits alone, rejected by the other Senators. He fled the city and raised an army, but was killed in battle.

Instead of a king, the Roman Republic was governed by officials called magistrates. Each year, Assemblies of the People elected new magistrates. The most important magistrates were the two Consuls. They were the heads of state and commanders-in-chief of Rome's armies. The two Consuls had equal power, so each could stop the other taking any action he did not like. To be made Consul was the highest honour available to a Roman citizen. In times of crisis, such as a foreign invasion, all power could be given to one man, called a dictator. But the dictator only held office for a limited time and a particular purpose.

The Consuls were guided by the advice of a council called the Senate which was made up of men who had been magistrates. People appointed to the Senate were members for life.

In principle, the government of the Republic seems democratic. The Senate existed only to give advice, and Assemblies of the People elected the magistrates, passed new laws and voted for war or peace. Every Roman citizen could vote in these assemblies.

In practice, however, most Romans had little political power. A citizen was a free, adult male, so women and slaves had no political rights at all. The election system was also biased against poor people, whose votes in the public assemblies were worth much less than the votes of the rich.

Magistrates were unpaid, so only wealthy people could stand for election. Moreover, rich men could often control the voting by bribery.

In fact, important decisions in Rome were made by the Senate; moreover most of Rome's magistrates, Senators, Consuls and generals came from the same few, wealthy families. This type of government, in which power is held by a small group of people, is called an oligarchy.

In the early years of the Republic, Rome's ruling families were all patricians. Patricians were people who could trace their ancestry back to the first Romans. They claimed that this gave them the right to rule. People who could not claim noble ancestry were called plebeians or commoners. Their parents were poor traders or farmers. Even if a plebeian was as rich as a patrician, he could not hold high office. Most plebeians were poor and the law gave them little protection.

Romans who could afford it had their portraits carved on their tombs. This carving shows a typical well-off family – Lucius Vibius, his wife Vecilia Hila and their son. Can you see the family resemblance?

For three hundred years, all but fifteen of Rome's Consuls came from the same few noble families. The outsiders were called 'new men' and they were distrusted by the nobility. One of them was a soldier called Marius. According to the historian Sallust, Marius made a speech attacking the nobility:

Compare me, the 'new man' with these high and mighty ones. They scorn my lack of illustrious [famous] ancestors, I scorn their idleness. The worst that can be said of me is that I am a man of humble background. If these men look down on me, they ought equally to look down on their own ancestors, who, like me, had no nobility but what they earned by their own merits. I cannot point to the portraits, triumphs or consulships of my ancestors. But I can show medals and other military honours, to say nothing of the scars on my body – all of them in front. These are my family portraits, these my title of nobility. (Sallust, *Jugurthine War*)

Why did it matter that Marius' scars were 'in front'?

Gradually, the plebeians demanded a share of power. In 494 BC, they appointed their own officials called tribunes. The tribune's role was to protect ordinary people from injustice, such as unfair arrest. So that he was always available, a tribune's doors were never closed. The plebeians swore to kill anyone who murdered a tribune. Eventually, tribunes gained the right to reject measures taken by the Consuls. Finally in 367 BC, it was decided that each year one of the two Consuls must be a plebeian.

Although these changes seemed to give political power to the plebeians, in fact Rome was still controlled by a few families. When a plebeian became a Consul, his family joined the nobility. Most of the tribunes shared the outlook of the ruling class too, because they usually came from rich families. Some patricians even had themselves adopted by plebeian families, just so that they could become tribunes. The Roman nobles allowed the most influential plebeians to join them, to strengthen their own position.

For most of the history of the Republic, there were no such things as political parties. The noble families in the Senate were able to govern Rome unchallenged. But by 100 BC, two groups had appeared. On one side were Romans called *populares* or 'men of the people'. These were politicians who appealed over the heads of the Senate directly to the people. Some of them were genuine reformers who

wanted to help the poor of Rome. Others simply wanted to use the people to advance their own careers. On the other side were people who called themselves *optimates*, the 'best men'. They were conservative, traditional Romans who wanted to preserve the power of the Senate. They were terrified of revolution. Each side claimed that it was defending liberty. Eventually, their conflict led to bloody civil wars – wars in which Roman fought against Roman.

Ordinary people, like these smiths, had few political rights.

The Civil Wars

A bust of Caius Marius, (155–86 BC), the ambitious general who was hated by Rome's nobility.

In the first century BC, a series of ambitious generals appeared in Rome. These men used military power to take control of the state. As a result, the republican method of government was destroyed in a number of civil wars.

The trouble started with the rivalry of two generals, Marius and Sulla. Marius came from a humble background and was hated by Rome's nobility. He was one of the *populares*, the men who looked to the people, rather than to the Senate, for power. In 107 BC, he was elected Consul, against the wishes of many Senators.

Marius set about reforming the way the Roman Army was recruited. Previously, it had been made up of farmers, people who would be conscripted (forced to serve) for a few years, but were eager to return to their farms. Marius now recruited an army of volunteers, mainly from the city poor. These volunteers were a new kind of professional soldier. What no one realized was that they would be loyal to their general, rather than to the state. They would be willing to kill fellow Romans if their general commanded it.

Marius' rival was the noble general, Sulla. He fought as Marius' lieutenant in Africa, and the two men came to hate each other. Because of his noble background, Sulla became a champion of the Senate. In 88 BC, the two generals clashed over a war that Rome was fighting against an eastern king called Mithridates. The Senate wanted Sulla to command in the war, but the People's Assembly voted for Marius. Furious, Sulla marched on Rome and captured it. Marius was forced to flee for his life. Then Sulla set off to fight Mithridates.

With Sulla out of the way, Marius returned to Rome. Supported by the *populares*, he set about massacring Sulla's noble followers. In 86 BC, Marius died. Two years later, Sulla returned to Rome with his army. He defeated the *populares* in battle and proclaimed himself dictator. Now it was Sulla's turn to take revenge. He drew up lists containing the names of his enemies. They were then hunted down and killed without trial. This process was called proscription. After two years, Sulla felt that the rule of the nobility was now safe. He retired, dying in 78 BC.

The conflict between the Senate and the *populares* broke out again twenty years later. Pompey, the champion of the Senate, had served under Sulla. Julius Caesar, the leader of the *populares*, had married Marius' niece.

Above *Lucius Cornelius Sulla (138–78 BC), an engraving from a coin issued after his death. Sulla was the first military leader to march on Rome at the head of an army. He wanted to restore the power of the nobility, but his example would be followed by later generals who aimed at power for themselves.*

Left *Julius Caesar (100–44 BC) was made dictator for life in 44 BC. However, he then had less than one year left to live.*

At first, Pompey and Caesar had worked together, helping each other get the most important military commands. Caesar was a brilliant general who was loved by his troops. Between 58 and 51 BC, he conquered northern Gaul and made expeditions to Germany and Britain. But as his reputation grew, he came to be feared by Pompey and the Senate. They tried to deprive him of his command. Then in 49 BC, Caesar crossed the River Rubicon with his army and marched over the border into Italy. It was illegal for a Roman general to enter Italy with an army without the Senate's permission.

Pompey and the Senators were forced to flee to Greece, where they prepared their own troops. In 48 BC, Caesar

¶ In 48 BC, two Roman armies, led by Pompey and Julius Caesar, fought each other at Pharsalus in northern Greece. The Greek historian, Plutarch, described the battle:

Here were opposed armies of the same kin, ranks of brothers, identical standards; here the whole manhood and might of a single state was involved in self-destruction – a clear lesson of how mad a thing human nature is when under the sway of a passion. If only Caesar and Pompey had been content quietly to govern, the greatest parts of the earth were theirs to control. Or if they still yearned for triumphs, they could have had all the wars they wanted with Parthians and Germans.

(Plutarch, *Lives*)

The Roman politician, Cicero, supported Pompey in the civil wars. After Pompey was defeated, Cicero wrote to a friend:

We foresaw the destruction of one of the two armies and its leader, a vast disaster. We realized that victory in civil war is the worst of all calamities. I dreaded the prospect, even if victory should fall to those we had joined. We live, it may be said, in a state that has been turned upside down.

(Cicero, *Letters*)

Why did people think that civil war was worse than any other kind of war?

A coin showing the two-headed Roman god of war and of new beginnings, Janus. Like Janus, the people of Rome were split in two by the civil wars.

defeated them at Pharsalus in northern Greece. Pompey escaped to Egypt, but was murdered there.

Back in Rome, Caesar was declared dictator for life. He filled the Senate with his own followers and began to reform the way the Empire was governed. He was given the right to have his portraits on Roman coins, the first time the privilege had been given to a living Roman. To many people, he seemed a king in all but name. A group of Roman nobles, led by Brutus and Cassius, plotted to kill Caesar and save the Republic. On 15 March 44 BC, they stabbed him to death in the Senate.

Caesar's murder did not save the Republic. Instead, it led to more years of civil war. His death was avenged by his adopted son, Octavian, and Mark Antony, one of his lieutenants. In 43 BC, Octavian marched to Rome at the head of an army and demanded the Consulship. As Sulla had done, Octavian and Antony now proscribed and killed their enemies. They defeated the republican leaders in battle at Philippi in Greece. Afterwards, Brutus and Cassius killed themselves.

The story of Rome's civil wars has inspired many writers, amongst them William Shakespeare. In this scene from a production of Shakespeare's Julius Caesar, *the assassins will shortly rush forward and stab the dictator to death.*

Right *In 40 BC, Octavian and Antony split the Roman Empire in two. Octavian ruled the western half from Rome; Antony ruled the eastern half with the Egyptian queen, Cleopatra. It was to be an uneasy partnership.*

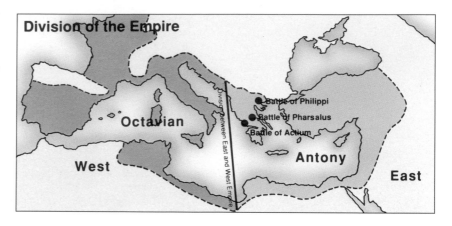

Division of the Empire

Battle of Philippi

Battle of Pharsalus

Battle of Actium

Octavian

West

Antony

East

Division between East and West Empire

Below *Historians believe that this sculpture shows a galley used in the Battle of Actium. The crocodile suggests that it is a scene of the River Nile.*

Octavian and Antony then divided the empire between them. Octavian ruled the west from Rome, Antony the east from Egypt. But they also quarrelled. Eventually, more fighting broke out, and in 31 BC, Octavian's fleet defeated Antony at the Battle of Actium. Antony committed suicide.

One by one, the claimants to power had been killed off. Only Octavian remained, the master of the Roman world. He became the most powerful Roman of them all.

The Roman Emperors

After years of civil war, the Romans longed for peace. In exchange for peace, they did not mind letting one man, Octavian, take power. He became Rome's first emperor and took on the name of Augustus.

Although he had sole power, Augustus did not call himself a king. He remembered that Julius Caesar had been murdered for acting like one, and did not want to share this fate. Instead, Augustus claimed that he was only the first citizen, or *princeps* of Rome. The Republic, he said, had been restored. The Senate actually had little real power, but Augustus made sure it kept its traditional prestige and respect. He won over the people of Rome by providing cheap food and public entertainment; he won over the army with extra pay. Having killed his enemies, he could now afford to be tolerant and easygoing, and lived simply. Under Augustus, Rome had forty-three years of peace and order. He had no son, grandsons nor nephews to succeed him.

Above *Rome's first emperor, Augustus, with his arm stretched out as if issuing commands to his troops. His breastplate shows a soldier recovering a Roman battle standard from an enemy. Augustus' statues always show him as a handsome young man.*

Left *This carving shows a charioteer who has just reached the turning posts at one end of the Circus Maximus. Chariot races were enormously popular.*

When Augustus died in AD 14, his stepson Tiberius took over as emperor. Tiberius had been a successful general and was a cautious ruler. But he could not manipulate people as well as Augustus. He was moody and difficult, and the Senators distrusted him. He hated wasting money, so he cut down on public entertainments. Tiberius also feared assassination: many Senators were accused of plotting against him, and they were forced to kill themselves. In AD 26, Tiberius retired to the island of Capri, where he felt safe. Although he ruled for eleven more years, he never returned to Rome. When he died, in AD 37, the people of Rome rejoiced.

Tiberius was followed by his great-nephew Gaius, nicknamed Caligula, which means 'little boots'. At first Caligula was hugely popular. But he was a completely irresponsible young man, who may well have been insane. Unlike Augustus and Tiberius, he did not even pretend that Rome was still a Republic. He treated the Senate with contempt. It was rumoured that he planned to make his favourite horse a Consul. He even declared that he was a god. After ruling for only four years, Caligula was murdered by the imperial guard, chiefly because he had been so cruel.

It is difficult to find out what the emperors were like. To learn about them we have to rely on Roman historians. But sometimes they contradict each other.

Velleius Paterculus was a soldier who served under Tiberius. He wrote a history of Rome while Tiberius was still alive. This is how he describes Tiberius' rule:

Who could tell in detail all the achievements of the last sixteen years? Right is now honoured, evil is punished. When was the price of grain more reasonable, or when were the blessings of peace greater? The emperor's generosity benefits whole cities. The best of emperors teaches his citizens to do right by doing it himself. Though he is greatest among us in authority, he is still greater in the example he sets.

(Velleius Paterculus, *Roman History*)

After Tiberius' death, a historian called Suetonius gave a very different version of his reign:

Tiberius was tight-fisted to the point of miserliness. He did many wicked deeds to gratify his lust for seeing people suffer. He would remark, 'Let people hate me, so long as they fear me!' Soon he broke out in every sort of cruelty and never lacked for victims.

(Suetonius, *The Twelve Caesars*)

Can you think of a reason why these two accounts are so different?

Left *This mosaic shows the famous poet Virgil, sitting between two of the muses – the goddesses who inspire writers. He holds his greatest work, the* Aeneid. *This poem tells the story of Aeneas, the legendary founder of the Roman race, but it also celebrates Virgil's patron Augustus.*

Below *This bronze statuette of Nero was found in Suffolk. It is based on statues of the famous Greek soldier-king, Alexander the Great. Nero was no soldier, but he loved playing different roles.*

The soldiers who killed Caligula proclaimed his uncle Claudius as emperor. Claudius ruled from AD 41 to 54. He made several reforms in the government of the Empire and he organized the invasion and conquest of Britain (AD 43). But people complained that he acted cruelly because he was dominated by his wives and by the freed slaves whom he made his civil servants.

Claudius' stepson, Nero, was only seventeen when he became emperor. Like Caligula, he was very popular to begin with but later earned people's hatred. His way of life shocked traditionally-minded Romans. He spent vast sums on luxurious living and built a huge palace in the centre of Rome. Nero believed he was the greatest poet, musician and charioteer alive. He loved performing for the public and even went on a musical tour of Greece. Nero also had many people murdered, including his mother, wife and half-brother. In AD 68, the Roman armies in Gaul and Spain rebelled against him. He was now so unpopular that no one would defend him. Nero killed himself. He was the last emperor from the family of Augustus.

Above *A coin of Vespasian, the general who became emperor at the age of sixty. The son of a tax collector, Vespasian was the first emperor from a humble background.*

Below *Hadrian's villa at Tivoli, outside Rome, was inspired by the architecture of places he had visited.*

Nero's death was followed by another civil war for power and AD 69 was known as the year of four emperors. Different armies proclaimed their own generals as emperor. The eventual victor was an old general called Vespasian, who ruled from AD 69 to 79. He was followed by his sons, Titus (AD 79–81) and Domitian (AD 81–96). Domitian was another bloodthirsty ruler who was eventually murdered.

The reigns of Caligula, Nero and Domitian showed that it was not wise to let one family supply all Rome's emperors. After Domitian, the next three emperors adopted the most able general in the army as son and emperor-to-be. These generals had already proved their ability; by adopting them, an emperor avoided the risk of civil war. The result was the successful rule of warrior emperors such as Trajan (AD 98–117) and Hadrian (AD 117–138). Under Trajan, the Empire grew to its largest size.

Many Roman historians concentrate on the lives of the emperors. But most people who lived throughout the vast empire were hardly affected by changes of ruler. They knew roughly what the emperor looked like; his face appeared on their coins and his statues could be seen in every city. But one emperor was much the same as another to them.

Daily Life

Poor Romans did not write books, so we know little about their daily life and experiences. But wealthy writers, like Pliny the Younger, left detailed descriptions of upper-class life in Roman towns.

The working day began at sunrise and ended at noon. The early morning was for paying and receiving visits. A rich man would be visited by his clients – these were poorer Romans who came to him for help and advice. For the rich man, it was a sign of importance to have a large number of clients. The rest of the morning might be spent in the law courts or in the Senate. A rich woman's morning might be

Public baths were an important social centre in every town. The baths at Bath, shown here, used water from a hot spring. People travelled to Bath from all over the Empire for the supposed healing property of the waters.

spent in household duties. She held the key to the household store and would issue daily supplies to the slaves. She might also spin wool and weave, though it was less common for rich people to do this kind of work by the time of Augustus.

After a light lunch, in summer there would be a siesta or afternoon sleep. It was followed by exercise, such as a ball game. Then men and women would relax separately at the public baths. There were cold, warm and hot baths, as well as a heated room for sweating, rather like a sauna. The Romans had no soap. Instead, an attendant would rub oil onto their bodies and scrape them with a tool called a strigil. The public baths were an important place to meet friends.

After the bath, there was the main meal of the day, beginning in late afternoon or early evening. At dinner, Romans would recline on couches and eat with their fingers.

Most of the wealth of Rome's upper classes came from the land. As well as a town house, rich Romans often owned a farming estate, or villa, in the country. The villa

A Roman marriage ceremony. Marriages were usually arranged by the fathers of the couple.

might produce corn, vines, olives, fruit or timber and it would be worked by slaves. Many villas were luxurious, with their own baths, mosaics, fountains and under-floor, or hypocaust, heating.

Under Roman law, the father of a family, or *paterfamilias*, had complete power over his wife and children. He even had the right to sell his children into slavery. His son could own no property in his own name. Even when the son grew up and had his own children, he was still under the control of his father. But sons were valued because they could carry on the family name. They might win fame for the family in war or politics.

In contrast, the birth of a daughter was seen as a misfortune. All a girl could look forward to was an arranged marriage. Girls were usually married between the ages of twelve and seventeen. New-born girls were even known to be abandoned on public rubbish dumps by their parents. However, abandoned children were often rescued and brought up to be slaves.

Gladiators fighting lions in the arena. One man has already fallen. Wild beasts, such as lions and elephants, were brought to Rome from Africa to entertain the public.

Pliny the Younger was a Roman writer who published his letters. In one of the letters that he sent to his mother-in-law he listed the many virtues of his wife:

She is highly intelligent and a careful housewife, and her devotion to me is a sure sign of her virtue. She keeps copies of my works to read again and again and even learn by heart. She has even set my verses to music and sings them, to the accompaniment of her lyre. All this gives me the highest reason to hope that our happiness will last for ever and go on growing. Please accept our united thanks for having given her to me and me to her as if chosen for one another.

(Pliny, *Letters*)

What qualities did Romans like Pliny expect in their wives?

The houses of wealthy Romans were full of colourful wall paintings and mosaics, often showing scenes of daily life. This painting shows the daughter of the house at her music lesson, watched over by her mother. The daughters of the rich were encouraged to learn musical instruments.

Left Many Romans had slaves to perform their household tasks. This bronze figure is a black slave, cleaning a boot.

The Roman life of leisure was made possible by slavery. Slaves were prisoners of war, bought in the market place, or the children of slave parents. Roman families preferred the second kind. They would grow up speaking Latin. They could be trained for a future job as a cook, a secretary or a tutor. Household slaves could become valued members of the family and might eventually be given their freedom. It was much worse to be a slave working in the quarries, mines or on the land. Their lives were hard and short. Other slaves were forced to become gladiators – people who fought to the death in the arena for the entertainment of the public.

Above This bronze tag was worn by a slave. It says, 'Hold me, lest I flee, and return me to my master Viventius on the estate of Callistus'.

Roman Religion

The Romans worshipped many gods and goddesses. They thought that the gods controlled their lives and they hoped to bring themselves good luck by pleasing the gods. Each god had special qualities. Many gods were the helpers and protectors of particular groups of people.

The most powerful god was Jupiter, who was worshipped as the protector of the city and the state. Juno was the protectress of married women and Minerva the goddess of craftsmen. Saturn was the god of farming and Mars the god of war.

To honour their gods, the Romans built many temples. Each temple contained a statue of the god, and was thought to be that god's home. The temples were looked after by priests, or pontiffs, who had to make sure that the gods were not offended. Temples were not places for group worship; but individual Romans would bring gifts to the temple to try to win the god's favour. They provided animals which were sacrificed in front of the temple. Each god had a feast day when people would hold processions and celebrations in the street.

Above *At the centre of each Roman temple stood a large statue of the god who was worshipped there. This is Minerva, goddess of arts and crafts.*

Right *A bull, a sheep and a pig are led in procession to an altar, where they will be sacrificed. The man whose head is covered is the pontiff, or priest. His assistant holds a box of incense.*

Many Romans were superstitious. The historian Suetonius described the superstitions of the Emperor Augustus:

He is recorded to have been scared of thunder and lightning, against which he always carried a piece of sealskin as a charm. Warnings given in dreams were not lost on him. He had absolute faith in certain signs which warned of the future: considering it bad luck to put his right foot in his left shoe as he got out of bed, but good luck to start a long journey or voyage during a drizzle of rain. He also had a superstition against starting a journey on the day after a market day.

(Suetonius, *The Twelve Caesars*)

Do people today share any of these, or similar, superstitions?

A bronze hand covered with magic symbols to ward off evil spirits. Hands such as these were offered to a god from Turkey called Sabazios.

Many Romans thought that the gods sent signs to show their wishes. These signs might appear in the flight of birds, or the way that sacred chickens ate their food. There were special priests called augurs who explained what the signs meant. Another group, the *haruspices*, interpreted the god's wishes by examining the organs of sacrificed animals. Marks on an animal's liver would show whether the god was pleased with the sacrifice. Signs and omens also announced great historical events. The writer Appian described dogs howling like wolves, showers of stones and continuous lightning on sacred temples; all fearful signs. Not all Romans believed in these signs. Marcus Porcius Cato (234–149 BC) said that he could not understand how two *haruspices* could pass in the street without grinning at each other!

A lararium, *or household shrine, where a Roman family would worship its gods. It is designed to look like a miniature temple. The two dancing figures holding drinking horns are the* lares. *The central figure is the spirit of the family. The snake, an earth spirit and a spirit of the house, eats offerings brought to an altar by the family each day.*

Some Roman historians believed that there were religious reasons for Rome's success. Rome had been able to conquer its neighbours because of the favour of the gods. The historian, Livy, wrote:

You will find that those who followed the gods had every success, while those who disregarded them were visited with misfortunes. (Livy, *History*)

After the disastrous civil wars in the first century BC, the poet, Horace, blamed the sufferings of the Romans on their neglect of the gods:

Roman, although you are innocent, you shall pay the penalty for your father's crimes – until you have restored the crumbling temples and statues of the gods, foul with black smoke.
(Horace, *Odes*)

Would modern historians agree with Horace and Livy? Do people today think that historical events are caused by the actions of gods?

The Romans believed that every household was protected by its own gods. Each house contained a shrine where the family worshipped its household gods – the *penates* who protected the store cupboard, and the *lares*, which were spirits of the house and fields. A fire was kept burning, sacred to Vesta, goddess of the hearth.

Just as people believed that they owed their good fortune to the gods, under the emperors, Romans also began to believe that their peace and prosperity were due to the emperor. The emperor was thought to have god-like qualities and could actually become a god after death. But it was only the more popular emperors, such as Augustus and Vespasian, who were worshipped after death.

In Greece and Egypt, the Roman emperor was worshipped as a god while he was still alive. These countries had a long tradition of worshipping their rulers; so emperor worship was a useful way of keeping the Greeks and Egyptians loyal to Rome. Only the mad emperor, Gaius Caligula, seems to have considered himself really a god.

As their Empire grew, the Romans came into contact with many foreign religions. They adopted some of the foreign gods – Cybele from Turkey, Mithras from Persia and Isis from Egypt. It was much harder for Rome to accept Christianity. The Christians said that there was only one god and refused to recognize any of the Roman gods. Because they denied Rome's gods, they were blamed for disasters, such as earthquakes and fires; people thought the gods had sent

The worship of the god Mithras was brought to Rome from Persia by soldiers and traders. Here Mithras, surrounded by signs of the zodiac, is shown killing a sacred bull. According to legend, the blood of the bull gave life to the earth.

Because they were persecuted by the Romans, the first Christians had to disguise their religious pictures. This mosaic of a dolphin wrapped around an anchor represents Christ on the cross. The fish are Christ's followers. The anchor, a fixed point in a stormy sea, was a Christian emblem of hope.

these disasters to punish the Christians. At first, the Christians were persecuted. But the new religion was attractive, partly because it promised an afterlife. Christianity slowly started to spread until, in the fourth century AD, Emperor Constantine was converted. Christianity then became the state religion.

The Emperor Constantine is baptised by Sylvester, the bishop of Rome. This painting was made in the Middle Ages and celebrates an important event in the history of the Christian church: the Roman Empire was now Christian.

The End of the Empire?

While the Roman Empire was still growing, it had a steady supply of wealth and slaves, captured from the newly-conquered territories. But in AD 117, the Empire reached its largest size. The supply of booty ended. The Romans now needed huge armies to defend their borders. These armies had to be fed and paid out of the Empire's own resources. As a result, people had to pay higher and higher taxes.

Between the fourth and fifth centuries, waves of foreign tribes swept across the Empire. Some came to plunder and destroy, others wanted to settle and share the Roman way of life.

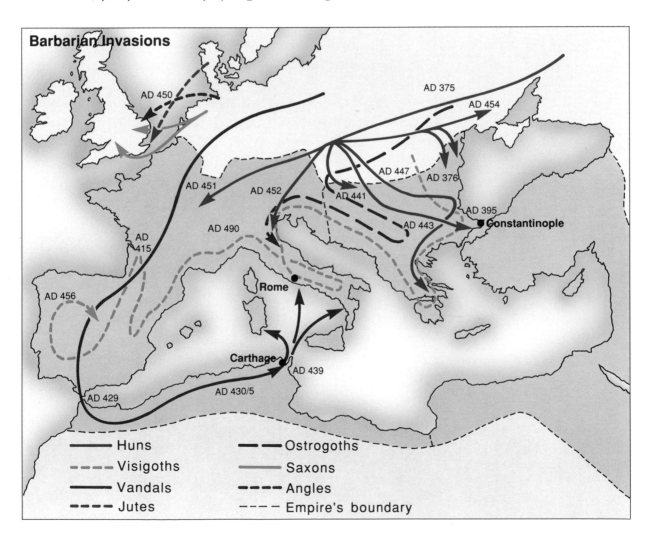

Barbarian Invasions

AD 450
AD 375
AD 454
AD 451
AD 452
AD 447
AD 376
AD 441
AD 395
AD 490
AD 443
Constantinople
AD 415
Rome
AD 456
Carthage
AD 439
AD 429
AD 430/5

Huns — Ostrogoths
Visigoths — Saxons
Vandals — Angles
Jutes — Empire's boundary

In AD 166, the Empire was devastated by a plague. Now there was a serious shortage of manpower as well as money. More and more, the Romans depended on foreigners, the *barbares* or barbarians, to man their armies. In particular, Rome recruited troops from German tribes living along the Empire's northern and eastern borders.

The huge armies were also a source of trouble. It became common for the armies to proclaim their own generals as emperor. Once again, the Empire was weakened by civil wars. Between AD 235 and 284, there were many emperors, almost all of whom died violent deaths. There was then a period of strong rule, under Diocletian (AD 284–305) and Constantine (AD 306–337), but it was not to last. After Constantine, the Empire was split in half, with two emperors, one in the east and one in the west.

The German tribes were attracted by the wealth and comfort of Roman life. Many of them had gradually been adopting Roman customs and lifestyles themselves. At the same time, they too were threatened by fiercer people from the east. In AD 370, the Huns, a warlike race from Asia, swept into Europe. They attacked the German tribes, forcing them to move westwards. The Romans gave shelter to one tribe, the Visigoths. But Romans and Visigoths soon came into

This mosaic from Carthage shows a Vandal leaving his villa. The Vandals enjoyed the comforts of the Roman way of life.

conflict. In AD 378, the Visigoths destroyed a Roman army and killed the eastern emperor, Valens.

Over the next fifty years, German tribes overran the western half of the Empire. The Visigoths invaded Italy, sacking Rome in AD 410. Then they moved on into France and Spain. They were followed by the Ostrogoths who settled in Italy. Another German tribe, the Vandals, plundered northern Europe and Spain. Then they crossed into north Africa. Meanwhile Angles and Saxons, tribes from northern Germany, crossed the sea and settled in Britain.

In the east, the Empire did continue, though it really became a Greek Empire. It was known as the Byzantine Empire, and its capital was at Constantinople. Greek, not Latin, was the language of the Byzantine Church and government.

After the German invasions in the west, the central government in Rome had less and less power. Gradually the Roman provinces became more independent. Yet the Roman way of life was still a powerful influence in western

The sixth-century church of St Vitale in Ravenna. The Church kept Rome's language and traditions alive during the Dark Ages.

The Domesday Book, the survey of Britain commissioned in 1086 by William the Conqueror. Like all legal records in the Middle Ages, it was written in Latin.

Europe. After all, the German tribes wanted to share in Roman life, not to destroy it: Vandal kings lived in luxurious villas like rich Romans; the Visigoths fought alongside Romans against the uncivilized Huns.

Roman traditions were also kept alive by the Church. Its head, the Pope, still lived in Rome. The German tribes were converted to Christianity, and through the whole of western Europe, Latin remained the language of the Church.

Many people continued to speak Latin, and it formed the basis for the Italian, French, Spanish, Portuguese and Romanian languages. In Britain, there was a bigger break with the Roman past. The German tribes, Angles and Saxons, brought their own language, English, which replaced Latin. None the less, over the years the English language borrowed hundreds of Latin words.

Up until the nineteenth century, educated Europeans were expected to understand Latin. It was an international language for science and scholarship. It provided terms for law and medicine. Animals and plants were classified with Latin names.

Latin has been a strong influence on the English language and you cannot go far without bumping into a Latin word. Many of them have come to English through French. Other Latin words were borrowed direct. Through Latin, some Greek words have entered the language too.

As an experiment, look at the last paragraph on page 42. How many of the words in it do you think came from Latin?

Now look at the paragraph again, reprinted below. All the words in **bold** are from Latin.

Up until the **nineteenth century**, **educated Europeans** [from Greek, through Latin] were **expected** to understand **Latin**. It was an **international language** for **science** and **scholarship** [from Greek, through Latin]. It **provided terms** for law and **medicine**. **Animals** and **plants** were **classified** with **Latin names**.

Today, we are still influenced by the Romans. We use the Roman alphabet. We use Latin abbreviations, often without realizing it: e.g. is short for *exempli gratia*; etc. is short for *et cetera*. British coins are not only modelled on Roman coins, they also have Latin phrases written on them. We still use the Roman calendar: January, March and June are named

Federal Hall in Manhattan, where the first US Congress met. Americans have modelled their architecture and their political system on the Roman Republic.

This dish, made in 1560, shows Caesar destroying a bridge at Geneva. Throughout history artists have been inspired by Roman subjects.

after the gods Janus, Mars and goddess Juno; July and August are named after Julius Caesar and Augustus; September, November and December are named after Roman numbers. The planets are also named after Roman gods and goddesses.

The Roman political system has also been influential. The government of the USA was modelled on that of the Roman Republic; the Americans set up a Senate and a House of Representatives, corresponding to Rome's Senate and Popular Assemblies. They even borrowed the Roman eagle on their emblem.

Until the twentieth century, poets and writers imitated Roman literature. Painters and sculptors used Roman themes. Architects copied Roman buildings; many banks and museums look like Roman temples. In the nineteenth century, people even built triumphal arches; Marble Arch in London and the *Arc de Triomphe* in Paris are both based on Roman models. Can you think of any other ways that the Roman past has influenced the way we live today?

Timeline

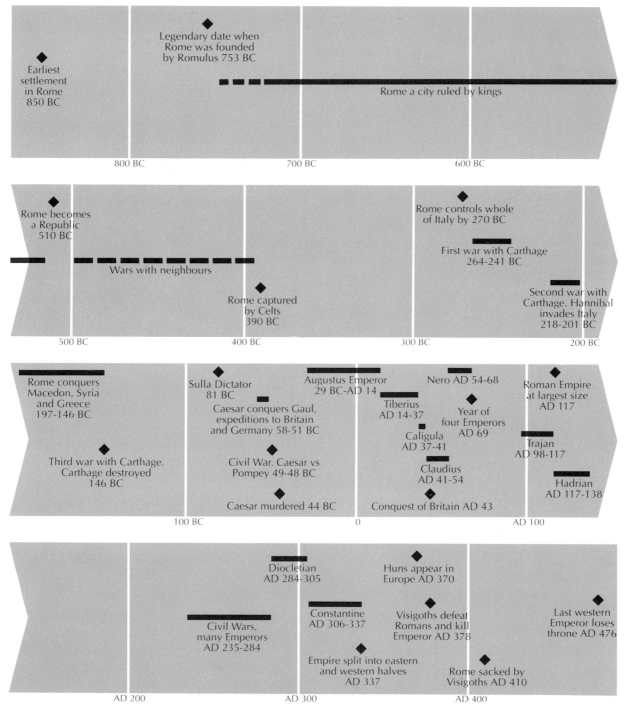

Earliest settlement in Rome 850 BC

Legendary date when Rome was founded by Romulus 753 BC

Rome a city ruled by kings

800 BC   700 BC   600 BC

Rome becomes a Republic 510 BC

Wars with neighbours

Rome captured by Celts 390 BC

Rome controls whole of Italy by 270 BC

First war with Carthage 264-241 BC

Second war with Carthage. Hannibal invades Italy 218-201 BC

500 BC   400 BC   300 BC   200 BC

Rome conquers Macedon, Syria and Greece 197-146 BC

Third war with Carthage. Carthage destroyed 146 BC

Sulla Dictator 81 BC

Caesar conquers Gaul, expeditions to Britain and Germany 58-51 BC

Civil War. Caesar vs Pompey 49-48 BC

Caesar murdered 44 BC

Augustus Emperor 29 BC-AD 14

Tiberius AD 14-37

Caligula AD 37-41

Claudius AD 41-54

Conquest of Britain AD 43

Nero AD 54-68

Year of four Emperors AD 69

Roman Empire at largest size AD 117

Trajan AD 98-117

Hadrian AD 117-138

100 BC   0   AD 100

Civil Wars, many Emperors AD 235-284

Diocletian AD 284-305

Constantine AD 306-337

Empire split into eastern and western halves AD 337

Huns appear in Europe AD 370

Visigoths defeat Romans and kill Emperor AD 378

Rome sacked by Visigoths AD 410

Last western Emperor loses throne AD 476

AD 200   AD 300   AD 400

45

Glossary

Alliance   An agreement or pact of friendship made between countries or peoples.

Assemblies of the People   Gatherings of Roman citizens in Rome for the purpose of voting.

Augurs   Priests who said they could tell the wishes of the gods, for example by watching the flight of birds.

Barbarians   Foreigners, people from outside the Roman Empire.

Byzantine Empire   The empire based in Constantinople that developed out of the eastern Roman Empire when the power of Rome declined.

Celts   A race of people who lived in what is now France, Spain, Britain and the Balkans. Their descendants still live in Brittany, Wales, Scotland and Ireland. Welsh and Irish are both Celtic languages.

Citizen   A member of a state. In Rome, only free men were citizens, with the right to vote. Neither women nor slaves were citizens.

Civil war   A war fought between people who live in the same country.

Clients   People who relied on the protection of someone who was more powerful; in return, they voted the way he told them and attended on him.

Colonies   Cities founded by the Romans in areas they conquered.

Consuls   The two chief magistrates of Rome, who held office for one year.

Democratic   Democratic governments are usually elected by the majority of people in a country. Everyone has a right to say how the country should be governed.

Dictator   A ruler with total power. Roman dictators were given power only for a limited period during an emergency, such as a foreign invasion.

Empire   A large area under the control of a single state.

Forum   The centre of a Roman town where public business took place.

Gladiator   A slave or criminal who had to fight to entertain the public.

Haruspices   People who claimed to interpret the wishes of the gods and tell the future by looking at the organs of sacrificed animals.

Huns   A warlike race of people from Asia who invaded Europe in the fourth century AD.

Hypocaust heating   A sort of central heating, where the heat comes up through the floor.

Lares   Roman spirits of the house and fields.

Legion   A part of the Roman army.

Magistrates   Roman government officials. They were elected each year by Assemblies of the People.

Maniple   A unit of the Roman army, consisting of around 120 men.

Oligarchy   Government by a small group of powerful people.

Optimates   The 'best men'. A group of traditional Senators who thought they had a right to rule Rome.

Ostrogoths   The eastern Goths, a German tribe that conquered Italy in the fifth and sixth centuries AD.

Paterfamilias   The father, and head, of a Roman family.

Patricians   Roman nobles who could

trace their families back to the earliest families in Rome.

Penates Roman gods of the store cupboard.

Phalanx A line of battle in tight formation.

Plebeians Romans who did not have noble ancestors.

Pontiff A Roman priest.

Populares The 'men of the people'. A political group that challenged the power of the Senate by appealing directly to the people.

Princeps The 'first citizen' of Rome, in other words, the emperor.

Proscription Making a list of people condemned to die. People who were proscribed were hunted down and killed without trial.

Republic A country without a king or emperor. The head of state is usually elected.

Senate Roman assembly made up of the heads of the leading families together with people who had been magistrates.

Strigil A tool used for scraping dirt off the body.

Tribunes Tribunes were officials who were elected to defend ordinary people, the plebeians, against injustice by the magistrates.

Vandals A German tribe that invaded France and Spain and settled in north Africa in the fifth century AD.

Villa A Roman country house, usually on a large farm or estate.

Visigoths The western Goths, a German tribe that invaded Italy and settled in France and Spain between the fifth and eighth centuries AD.

Books to Read

Books about the Romans

Peter Connolly, *Pompeii*, Oxford University Press, 1990.

Peter Connolly, *The Roman Army*, Simon and Schuster Young Books, 1989.

Mike Corbishly, *The Roman World*, Kingfisher, 1986.

F. R. Cowell, *Everyday Life in Ancient Rome*, Batsford, 1961 (hardback); Carousel, 1975 (paperback).

O. A. W. Dilke, *The Ancient Romans. How They Lived and Worked*, David and Charles, 1975.

Simon James, *Ancient Rome (Eyewitness Guides)*, Dorling Kindersley, 1990.

Martin O'Connell, *Roman Britain*, Wayland 1989.

Mike Rosen, *The Journeys of Hannibal*, Wayland 1990.

Books by Ancient Authors

Plutarch, *Fall of the Roman Republic*, Penguin Classics, 1958. Includes lives of Marius, Sulla, Caesar and Pompey. Plutarch was a great storyteller and these lives are full of dramatic incidents.

Suetonius, *The Twelve Caesars*, Penguin Classics, 1957. Entertaining biographies of Rome's first emperors, full of scandal and gossip.

Index

Picture acknowledgements

The author and publisher would like to thank the following: C. M. Dixon 6 (both), 7, 9 (bottom), 28 (bottom), 34 (top), 36, 38 (top); Mary Evans Picture Library 5, 21 (top); Michael Holford cover, 15, 22, 27, 30, 32, 33 (both), 35, 37, 40; Hulton Picture Company 20, 21 (bottom), 25 (top), 34 (bottom); The Mansell Collection 10, 11, 13, 16, 17, 19, 24, 27, 31, 38 (bottom); Public Record Office 42; Ronald Sheridan 8, 9 (top), 14, 25 (bottom), 28 (top), 29, 41, 44; Topham 23, 43. All artwork is by Peter Bull.